First
Facts®

Who Lived Here?

ARCTIC
Communities
PAST and PRESENT

by Cindy Jenson-Elliott

Consultant:
Zoe Burkholder, PhD
Assistant Professor, College of Education
and Human Services
Montclair State University
Montclair, New Jersey

CAPSTONE PRESS
a capstone imprint

First Facts are published by Capstone Press,
1710 Roe Crest Drive, North Mankato, Minnesota 56003
www.capstonepub.com

Library of Congress Cataloging-in-Publication Data
Cataloging information on file with the Library of Congress.
978-1-4765-4060-3 (library binding)
978-1-4765-5142-5 (paperback)
978-1-4765-5995-7 (eBook PDF)

Editorial Credits
Brenda Haugen, editor; Juliette Peters, designer; Svetlana Zhurkin,
media researcher; Charmaine Whitman, production specialist

Photo Credits
Alamy: North Wind Picture Archives, 17; Bridgeman Art Library: State
Central Navy Museum, St. Petersburg/Fur Traders of the Russian-
American Company, Igor Pavlovich Pshenichny, 15; Corbis: National
Geographic Society/Louis Agassi Fuertes, 11; Getty Images: Time
Life Pictures/Taro Yamasaki, 19; Library of Congress, cover (igloo);
National Geographic Creative: Roy Andersen, 5 (back), Tom Lovell, 13,
Victor R. Boswell, Jr., 9; Newscom: Visual&Written, 21; Shutterstock:
BMJ, 7, Dmytro Pylypenko, cover (middle back), 1, 2, 23, 24, Samiah
Samin (background), cover and throughout, Stasys Eidiejus, 5 (inset);
SuperStock: Alaska Stock/Design Pics, cover (left)

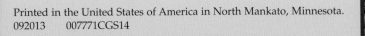
Printed in the United States of America in North Mankato, Minnesota.
092013   007771CGS14

TABLE OF CONTENTS

STONE AGE MIGRANTS

10,000 BC TO 2000 BC

People first came to the bone-chilling Arctic from the Asian region of Siberia. They traveled across the Bering Strait land bridge. They brought small, carved stone tools for hunting, cutting meat, and cleaning animal hides. In the Arctic, they **migrated** from west to east on foot, following animal herds. By 2000 BC people lived all across the Arctic.

---

migrate—to move from one place to another, often in search of food

Stone Age hunters look for food.

SIBERIA

RUSSIA

land bridge

Barrow

Nome

ALASKA

Bering Sea

THE FIRST COMMUNITIES

2000 BC

In 2000 BC Arctic people lived in groups of 15 to 20. Most families had two or three children. In the summer the people trapped and speared fish in **weirs**. During the fall they hunted musk oxen and caribou with bows and arrows. Fur clothes kept the people warm during the winter months. They ate food they had saved from their fall hunts.

---

weir—a trap that blocks fish from moving up or down a stream

Caribou were an important food source in the Arctic.

EXTREME CONDITIONS

Life in the Arctic can be extreme. In winter, the North Pole does not face the sun, so the Arctic sky is dark for two months. Temperatures can drop to minus 50 degrees Fahrenheit (minus 46 degrees Celsius). The sea freezes and forms thick slabs of ice.

NEW TOOLS AND HOMES

100 BC

Hunters used tools to catch animals to feed and clothe their families in 100 BC. Groups of hunters with spears chased caribou into traps made from stones. Hunters used ivory knives to cut holes in sea ice. Through the holes they speared seals.

During dark winter months, people stayed in houses made of logs, mud, and grass. The homes were warmed by stone fireplaces.

FACT

Women used curved knives called ulus to clean animal skins. They used ivory needles to sew the skins together and make clothes.

Hunters used tools made of ivory and stone.

HUNTERS IN BOATS AND ON DOGSLEDS

AD 1000

Warmer weather melted the sea ice around AD 1000. Whales crossed the Arctic Ocean. Whale hunters followed in **kayaks** and **umiaks**. The hunters depended on whales and seals for survival. They ate the meat and burned the fat in stone oil lamps for light and warmth. The hunters used the animals' rib bones as sled **runners**.

---

kayak—a covered, narrow boat that holds one person

umiak—a skin-covered whale hunting boat that holds about 20 people

runner—the long, narrow part of an object that allows it to move or slide

DOGS HELP WITH HUNTING

The whale hunters also used dogsleds. Dogs and dogsleds allowed the Thule people to travel and hunt more successfully than other groups from AD 1000 to 1600. Dogs could smell seals hiding under the ice. They would bark at holes to alert hunters. After a hunt teams of dogs pulled seals and whales across the snow.

NORSE SETTLERS ARRIVE

1200

Warmer temperatures brought people from Norway to parts of the Arctic in 1200. Thousands of Norse settlers came with sheep for wool, cows for milk, and farm tools. They traded iron and copper tools for ivory and polar bear **pelts** from the **native** people. When temperatures dropped, they went back to Norway and trade ended.

pelt—an animal's skin with the hair or fur still on it

native—people who originally lived in a certain place

Norse settlers bring sheep and cattle to the Arctic.

THE RUSSIAN FUR TRADE

1780s

In the 1780s Russian people traveled to the western Arctic in boats to trade with the native people. The Russians brought iron and copper tools and tobacco. They traded the goods for sea otter and polar bear pelts.

FACT

Russian **missionaries** also came to the Arctic in the late 1700s. The missionaries traveled to the Arctic to teach their religion to the native people.

missionary—a person who works on behalf of a religious group to spread the group's faith

Russian fur traders land in the Arctic.

AMERICAN WHALING

Whaling ships and salmon fishing boats from the United States worked along the Arctic **coast**. The Americans brought metal tools and guns to the Arctic. They also brought wood to build houses.

Arctic people began forming larger, permanent communities instead of following animals. They ate new foods, such as molasses. Their children went to school to learn English.

---

coast—land next to an ocean or sea

16

Boat crews attack a whale in the cold waters.

OIL AND MILITARY BASES
MID-1900s

More Americans came to the Arctic in the mid-1900s. They built **military** bases in the Arctic to watch Russia and keep the United States safe. Arctic oil discoveries brought thousands of people to drill oil wells and build roads. Many native people worked in these jobs. They no longer relied just on hunting and fishing. People traveled by snowmobile and lived in towns with stores and electricity.

---

military—the armed forces of a state or country

A WARMING ARCTIC

2000s

Rising temperatures are melting Arctic sea ice. Scientists studying **climate** change live beside oil workers and native families. But native people have kept their **traditions**. They hunt and fish. They use snowmobiles to travel, but they also use dogsleds.

BLENDING THE OLD WORLD WITH THE NEW ONE

The native Arctic people value traditions, but that does not mean they don't try new things. Today they work in jobs that were not choices for them long ago. These jobs include mining and **tourism**.

climate—the usual weather that occurs in a place

tradition—a custom, idea, or belief passed down through time

tourism—the business of taking care of visitors to a country or place

Bowhead whales are one of the Arctic people's most important food sources. At 45 feet (13.7 meters) long, bowheads are the world's second largest whales. They are believed to live between 100 and 200 years. Scientists think that living in cold temperatures may help them live longer.

GLOSSARY

climate (KLY-muht)—the usual weather that occurs in a place

coast (KOHST)—land next to an ocean or sea

kayak (KYE-ak)—a covered, narrow boat that holds one person

migrate (MYE-grate)—to move from one place to another, often in search of food

military (MIL-uh-ter-ee)—the armed forces of a state or country

missionary (MISH-uh-nair-ee)—a person who works on behalf of a religious group to spread the group's faith

native (NAY-tiv)—people who originally lived in a certain place

pelt (PELT)—an animal's skin with the hair or fur still on it

runner (RUHN-ur)—the long, narrow part of an object that allows it to move or slide

tourism (TOOR-i-zuhm)—the business of taking care of visitors to a country or place

tradition (truh-DISH-uhn)—a custom, idea, or belief passed down through time

umiak (OO-mee-ak)—a skin-covered whale hunting boat that holds about 20 people

weir (WEER)—a trap that blocks fish from moving up or down a stream

READ MORE

Doak, Robin S. *Arctic Peoples.* First Nations of North America. Chicago: Heinemann Library, 2012.

Dwyer, Helen, and Michael Burgan. *Inuit History and Culture.* Native American Library. New York: Gareth Stevens Pub., 2012.

Morris, Neil. *Living in the Arctic.* World Cultures. Chicago: Raintree, 2008.

INTERNET SITES

FactHound offers a safe, fun way to find Internet sites related to this book. All of the sites on FactHound have been researched by our staff.

Here's all you do:

Visit *www.facthound.com*

Type in this code: 9781476540603

Super-cool stuff!

Check out projects, games and lots more at
www.capstonekids.com

CRITICAL THINKING USING THE COMMON CORE

1. Look at the sidebar "Dogs Help With Hunting" on page 11. What is the author trying to explain in this sidebar? (Craft and Structure)

2. How have native people kept their traditions in modern times? (Key Ideas and Details)

INDEX